# MARX *versus* TOLSTOY

# MARX *versus* TOLSTOY

## A DEBATE

CLARENCE S. DARROW

ARTHUR M. LEWIS

CHICAGO
CHARLES H. KERR & COMPANY
CO-OPERATIVE

# PREFACE

This discussion treats an important question that has received no specific and thorough examination elsewhere, notwithstanding its gravity. Mr. Darrow is probably the foremost of the American representatives of the non-resistance theory, and his case is stated in these pages more pointedly and forcibly than in any of his published works. The arguments launched against Mr. Darrow will, I think, satisfy the opponents of the non-resistance philosophy.

ARTHUR M. LEWIS.

Chicago, Mar. 21, 1911.

DARROW'S FIRST SPEECH

# Marx versus Tolstoy: A Debate

## DARROW'S FIRST SPEECH

As this is a Sunday morning, and a semi-religious question, I take for my text the 38th and 39th verses in the 5th chapter of Matthew. I cannot quote it literally. It is quite a time since I have read it. But I know the import of it.

"Ye have heard that it hath been said," I am quoting from Matthew, "An eye for an eye, and a tooth for a tooth. But I say unto you: Resist not evil. But whosoever shall smite you on the right cheek, turn to him the other also."

I do not quote this because Matthew wrote it. I really do not know whether he did or not; and I care a great deal less. I could not find out whether Matthew wrote it, unless I should read Professor Foster's works on religion, and that would take too long. But I quote it because throughout all the Western world this has been the accepted statement of the doctrine of non-resistance. It is, perhaps, as good a statement of that theory as one can find in a few short sentences. Matthew had no patent on it, of course. There are very few thoughts in this world that are patented, and those are not worth it. It was undoubtedly very old before Matthew lived—if he lived. And it has been repeated a great many times since he died—if he died.

The theory of non-resistance is taken, generally, as the opposite to the theory of punishment, or the theory of vengeance, which, up to the time of the Christian religion, was the theory of the world—and since that time has been doubly the theory of the world. Its announcement, as generally admitted by those who have written and spoken upon the subject, has reference, first, to the treatment of those whom society calls criminals; next, perhaps, to governments in their relations to each other and to their subjects; and then to women and children, insane, prisoners, and the like. It relates to the way those who have the power have generally exercised that power in relation to the rest of the world.

Now, I might say in the beginning that I am not quite sure of this theory, or of any other theory. I used to be a good deal more positive than I am today. And, especially, I am

not at all sure that there is any
theory in philosophy, or morals (or
laws), that works out in sociology.
The science of society, if there is
such a science, is not an exact science.
You cannot demonstrate any theory
of society the way you can demonstrate the multiplication table, unless it is Socialism—and you cannot
demonstrate that in the same way
unless you are speaking to an audience of Socialists. You might demonstrate Single Tax to a Single
Taxer, but you could not do it to
anybody else. Exact science has little
to do—something to do, but little to
do—with the ways in which man or-
ganizes himself on the planet. He
does not move in straight lines, or
in regular curves, or even in crooked
lines, that can be depended upon.
When he learns what the crooked

line is he goes straight. And no theory of life, no theory of society can be worked out as to communal life, in the same way that you can work out the science of mathematics, or of astronomy, or geology, or any science dealing with anything that keeps still.

But the question is, whether the theory of punishment, as opposed to the theory of non-resistance, is most in harmony with life, and tends to the progress of the world; whether human life in its slow evolution is going toward the theory of non-resistance, or is going toward the theory of violence, and force, and punishment.

If one looks back at the origin of the State we do not find that it had the immaculate birth that most people believe. It was born in force and violence. The strong took a club, and made a state for himself. It was a simple state, kept there by the force of the strong man's club and his will. From that it has gone on until it takes a good many strong clubs, together with a good many armies, navies, policemen, lawyers, judges, etc., to keep the state in order. But through it all has run the theory of force, and through it all the power has come not from the people who asked it, but from the people who took it because they were the stronger. In the beginning the chief preserved order and the law, by saying what should be the law and enforcing order himself with his club.

In modern society the controlling forces arrange things as they want them, and provide that certain things are criminal. Sometimes those things have a semblance of natural crime, and sometimes not. The largest number of crimes are crimes against property. Sometimes you may trace them more or less directly to violation of some law that is in the natural world. But the fact is that the class which rules society come together and say what men must do, and what they must not do. And the man who violates it commits crime.

There are in society, and always have been, a large number of people, due mainly to conditions of society, who are what we call defectives; who are anti-social in their nature; whose life and conduct tend toward the disintegration of society, instead of the life of society. Very largely the treatment of crime is a question of treatment of these anti-social individuals. It is a question of treatment of those who persevere, in one way or another, in violating the rules of the game which society has made.

Way back under the Mosaic Law —and Moses did not have a patent on it either, but under the law of the world, the doctrine of an "Eye for an eye, a tooth for a tooth," prevailed. If a man killed another his life should be taken. If he stole something he should be punished. If he burglarized, then it meant something else, generally death. If he did something, the world would do something to him. And they would do that something that the world at that time thought was the right thing to do to him. In this way, even down to a hundred years ago, there were in England about two hundred crimes punishable by death. Almost everything that could be conceived was punished by death. And the lawyers, and judges, and preachers of that day had no thought that society could hang together if men were not hanged regularly for stealing sheep and anything that happened. The old doctrine of an eye for an eye, and a tooth for a tooth, was the common doctrine of the world, and that doctrine prevails today.

All penal codes are really built upon that doctrine. When you trace penal codes back to the beginning, they mean one thing, and only one, i. e., vengeance. A man has done something. He has caused some one to suffer. Therefore society will do something to him. In the early stages, if some one slew another, the members of his tribe had the right to go and take the life of any member of the other tribe in return. It did not matter whether he had been guilty or not. It was the law of vengeance, the law of punishment—and punishment and vengeance have always meant the same thing in the world, no matter where it has been.

Punishments of crimes have always been arbitrary. One man would say that for stealing a horse the somebody stealing it should go to jail for thirty days. Another would say that he should go to the penitentiary for a year; another would say five years; and somebody else would say he should be hanged by the neck until dead. Punishments have never depended upon the act done, but upon the man who saw the act done and the mind possessed by the ruling power. Of half a dozen judges given **authority** to administer punishment for a certain act no two judges would administer the same kind of punishment. One would say thirty days, another thirty years; just according to the mind he has. Some judge might give you less after breakfast than he would before. And another judge might give you more if he had attended a banquet through the small hours in the morning preceding, and did not feel well when he administered the sentence. All those things enter into it, and when you come to sum it all up, the real theory of it is a question of vengeance: The individual has done something. How much shall we do to him in return? How much will we make him suffer, because he has made some one else suffer?

Now, the non-resistant says, there is no such thing as crime, i. e., some of them say that. And they say that all punishment is bad, not heavy punishment alone—but all punishment; that man has no right to punish his fellow man, that only evil results from it; that the theory of vengeance and the theory of punishment is wrong; that it cures nobody, it does not tend to benefit society, it does not tend to change the defective, it does not tend to build up society. It is wrong and untrue in its whole theory; and the theory of non-resistance is the true theory as to crime. Whatever you may think of the theory, the world has been steadily going that way. It has been abolishing the death penalty, until today in most civilized countries there are only one or two crimes punishable by death; and it is very rarely that death is meted out for those.

Punishment has been growing less severe, and the methods of inflicting punishment are less severe. Of course, in the old day when men were less squeamish and more honest they had their hangings in broad daylight. Today we do not do it, not because we are better, but because we are squeamish. We have hangings in the jail, so that the effects of the punishment will be entirely lost to the community.

Our terms of imprisonment are not so long. Our methods of treating the imprisoned are more humane. We sentence a man to prison. Of course, in the old time he used to be put into a vile place, where he would be half clad and half fed, and where he would be covered with rags full of vermin, and where he would suffer all sorts of physical pain. Today we send him to jail, and we have the jail steam heated and electric lighted. We have a doctor to take care of him if so, perchance, the penalty is death he won't dies before his time comes; and if he is to be hanged he gets better food.than he ever did before. So far as men are entrusted with the power of carrying out these provisions they do it as humanely as they can do it.

In the old times the insane were treated like criminals. They were locked up in cells; they were loaded with chains; they WERE criminals, because the rest of the world did not understand them. We have gotten over that. We have learned to treat them as human beings, and to treat them as those suffering from ailment, whereas once in the history of the world they were visited with the old law of vengeance, the law of force. The world some time will learn to treat all of its defectives, and all those who violate the code, the same as they treat the insane and the ill today. And we are learning it, more and more, every day.

The theory of non-resistance does not, necessarily, say that a man cannot be restrained, although very likely that would not be necessary under any decent law of society. It is possible there are some who are so born, and have been so treated by society, that they would need to be restrained just as those afflicted with small-pox may be restrained in a hospital. But to restrain them and treat them until cured is one thing; to say that men because of some inherent wickedness deserve punishment is another thing. It would be absurd to restrain men suffering from small-pox and turn them out from a hospital in six weeks, whether cured or not. If hospitals were run in the same way as jails, we would send them up for thirty days; and if they got well in a week we would keep them there.

The whole theory of punishment, so far as there is any theory in it— and there is not much in it, except the idea of vengeance—but the whole theory, so far as there is one, comes from the religious conception; that some people are made inherently bad, that their minds are evil, or their souls for that matter, or whatever is the intangible thing about them that makes them evil. And they deserve punishment, because they have a "wicked, abandoned and malignant heart." We always have to put that "wicked, abandoned and malignant heart" in the indictment; otherwise it is no good. If he has that in his heart he can be punished. When twelve jurors and a judge get together, how can they tell whether his heart is bad or not? You could tell better if you dissect him. It goes upon the theory that man is apart from all the other beings that inhabit the universe; that he is a free moral agent; that he is a sort of a wild train running at large through the universe; that he is not governed by rules and conditions like the rest of the universe about us. But that the Lord created him, put a mind in him, a good heart in some of them; a wicked, abandoned and malignant heart in others; and sent them out to run wild independent of all the universe about them. And whenever

the good people catch up with these
wicked, abandoned and malignant
people then we punish the wicked
because, intrinsically, they are bad,
because they chose the evil instead of
the good. They could do better if
they wanted to be better, but they did
not choose. Society sends them to
jail, just as brutal parents whip their
children because they are bad instead
of good.

As a matter of fact, science and
evolution teach us that man is an animal, a little higher than the other
orders of animals; that he is governed by the same natural laws that
govern the rest of the universe; that
he is governed by the same laws that
govern animal life, aye, and plant
life; that free moral agency is a
myth, a delusion, and a snare. It
teaches us that he is surrounded by

environment, the product of all the
past, the product of all the present;
that he is here just like any other
subject of natural law; and that it is
not goodness, it is not badness, that
makes him what he is. It is the condition of life in which he lives. And
if he lives unwisely, if he is a defective, if he is anti-social, it is not that
he chose it; but it is due to a thousand conditions over which he has
not the slightest control. And the
wise society seeks to change his environment, to place him in harmony
with life. They know that they can
only change the man by changing the
conditions under which he lives; that
good and evil, so far as he is con-
cerned, do not exist; that right and
wrong are religious myths; that it is
a question of the adaptability of the
individual to social life, and a grad-

ual change of the environment under which he lives.

With the state is the same thing. The theory of force and violence applied to the state has drenched the world in blood. It has built great navies, and great armies. One nation builds a great navy and a great army, and destroys the resources of its people to build armies and navies. And another nation must build a greater navy and a greater army, because of the first. It makes of the nations of the earth armed camps, and the stronger the one arms itself, the stronger must the rest. England builds her wonderful navy out of the toil of the poor, out of what should buy food for the men who produce it. And when she builds it, then Germany must build one as large, and so must France, and so must

Russia build one, too. And of course patriotic America must build one. We need a navy for fear that a band of Senegambians might send a fleet to devastate Chicago some night. The theory of force and violence as applied to political states has built up the navies and armies of the world, and has caused most of the bloodshed of the human race. Is there any doubt but what nations would be stronger if they burned their battleships instead of building new ones? Can you increase the power of one nation by building ships, when you simply make others build larger? You never change the relative proportion, which alone makes the strength. If instead of adding to the navies the world over, we gradually got rid of them, the relative strength would be what it was before.

In industrial life it is the same thing. The reign of force, and the reign of violence, means competition, means industrial strife; is responsible for the greed and selfishness and avarice for the fortunes of the great and the poverty of the poor. It is only in these later days, when the world is looking to something better, when they are learning that force and violence is wrong, that it is wrong that merchants compete and cut each other's throats and workmen compete against each other to show how much less they can work for; and that it is better to organize society on a co-operative basis where each man is to help his fellowman instead of fighting his fellowman.

The dreams of the world may be far off, and we must fit every dream to every reality. For the world is imperfect. But if, as society progresses, there shall one day be a civilization better than the world has known, it will be a society where force and violence and bloodshed and cruelty have disappeared. It will be a world of brotherhood. A world not of destruction, of competion, of violence, of hatred, of enmity; but a world of co-operation, of mutual help, of love, of brotherliness; and that alone makes for the progress of the world.

# LEWIS' FIRST SPEECH

## LEWIS' FIRST SPEECH

Mr. Chairman, Mr. Darrow, Ladies and Gentlemen:

You will hear from me a very different theory of non-resistance to the one which has just been presented. If I believed that the theory of non-resistance had been properly stated this debate would close at this point, because I have heard next to nothing from the lips of my opponent with which I am not thoroughly in harmony. Mr. Darrow is probably the first man to treat this subject as if it were a department of modern criminology, as if it were a matter of penal codes, a question of the punishment of criminals, their treatment in general, and the treatment of the sick, the insane, etc. These are tacked on to the theory by my opponent, but they are only indirectly related to the question. In all that relates to the question of punishment of criminals I am in agreement with Mr. Darrow.

The subject of this debate is the theory expressed in the words: "Resist not evil." What is "evil"? Does it consist chiefly in the deeds performed by criminals, as my opponent seems to think? The criminal, according to Mr. Darrow, is not responsible for what he does; the evil goes further back than the criminal; it does not consist of what the criminal does, but of the causes which lead the criminal to do as he does. What are those causes? Let us go back to the causes of crime.

It will be agreed, I have no doubt,

by my opponent, and I shall maintain
it whether he agrees or not, that the
criminal is the product of society,
that is, the product of a society
which, through the instrumentality
of private property in the means of
life, shuts out some men from the
opportunity to live honestly and de-
cently. This is the prolific cause of
criminals. Whatever evil there may
be in crime must, in my opinion, be
laid not to the criminal, but at the
door of society, especially at the door
of the ruling class, the existence of
which is responsible for the criminal.
And the question of "Resist not evil"
in this field is not, shall society resist
the actions of the criminal whom it
has itself produced, but shall men
who have been shut off from the
means of life resist the society which
has so shut them off? Shall they re-

sist the ruling class which has monopolized their means of life, and left them face to face with starvation? Shall that ruling class—the existence of which is the real evil in the problem—be resisted? This is the question of resisting evil in my use of the terms. And I say, yes; we should resist this evil to the point of its abolition.

I am going to give you another exposition of the origin of the theory, or doctrine, of "Resist not evil." This theory, like all other theories, has what the philosophers would call a sufficient reason, or, as the scientists would term it, an efficient cause. Sufficient reason and efficient cause are back of all things. This is true of all theories, without regard to whether they are true or false. In fact, we can only judge the merit of a theory when we know its cause. Theories do not drop out of the clouds. They are not communicated to men by divine persons who live outside the universe. They cannot be accounted for on the ground of spontaneous generation. Theories grow out of the world of material reality, and social theories grow out of social phenomena.

The causes for the theory, put forward by Mr. Darrow, are hazy and indistinct and lack historical precision. They do not go back to the origin of the theory itself. This omission on the part of my opponent I shall proceed to remedy. He has given us the names of the men who are responsible for this theory—Jesus Christ and His disciples, etc. I shall endeavor to give you the forces and conditions which caused the theory to be impressed upon the minds of the men who taught it.

It is generally supposed that progress is universal. So far from this being the case, the majority of the human race do not even understand the idea of progress. If it is explained to them they treat it with contempt. This is the mental attitude of all the people of the Orient. And this attitude the Orientals held in common with the ancients and with savages. Herbert Spencer, in his "Principles of Sociology," says:

"Primitive man is conservative to a degree. Even on contrasting the higher races with one another, and even on contrasting different classes in the same society, it is observable that the least developed are the most averse to change."

Walter Bagehot, in his brilliant

little book, "Physics and Politics," maintains:

"Our habitual instructors, our ordinary conversation, our inevitable and ineradicable prejudices, tend to make us think that 'progress' is the normal fact in human society, the fact which we should all expect to see, the fact which we should all be surprised if we did not see. But history refutes this. The ancients had no conception of progress; they did not even so much as reject the idea, they did not even entertain the idea. Oriental nations are just the same now. Since history began they have always been what they are."

And the greatest of all authorities on this question, Sir Henry Sumner Maine, says:

"Vast populations, some of them with a civilization considerable but peculiar, detest that which in the language of the West would be called Reform. The entire Mohammedan world detests it. The multitudes of colored men who swarm the great continent of Africa detest it, and it is detested by that large part of mankind which we are accustomed to leave on one side as barbarous and savage. The millions and millions of men who fill the Chinese Empire loathe it (and what is more) despise it. \* \* \* The enormous mass of the Indian population dreads change. \* \* \* To the fact that enthusiasm for change is comparatively rare must be added the fact that it is extremely modern. It is known but to a small part of mankind, and to that part but for a short period during a history of incalculable length."

This opposition to change, which is dominant in the Oriental world, is responsible for the stagnation of the East.

Now, this stagnation is not without a cause, and the cause is not far to seek. We have only to read their literature and to examine their re-

ligions. These two are really one—
the great bulk of their literature is
religious. The greatest and most
widespread of these religions is that
of Prince Gautama Buddha—Buddhism. Today this faith rules the
minds of five hundred million men,
or one-third of the entire human
race. It has enough in common with
all the other Oriental religions to
typify them all.

The first and most fundamental of
the truths of Buddhism is one called
the "First of Four Noble Truths."
Four truths make up the system.
That first truth is, that "everything
is Misery." The ruling principle of
the universe is evil. You cannot be
protected and guarded from evil.
It is inherent in all things. It cannot
be escaped, it cannot be eradicated, it
cannot be changed. It is the absolute

and supreme law of the universe. This is the first great dogma of the Buddhist religion.

The logical consequence of this belief in the supremacy of evil is that the word "sorrow" is a great word in the Buddhist faith. In fact, the faith itself is summed up in the word "sorrow."

The second of these noble truths is "Sorrow's Cause," or the "Cause of Sorrow." What is this thing that is the Cause of Sorrow? In the estimation of the Orientals it is the thing modern sociologists call "desire"— the desire to escape and to overcome oppression; the desire to conquer evil, and to put in its place happiness and joy. The desire to do this is the one damnable thing in the estimation of the Oriental. He believes that evil is so supreme that any attempt to resist it is a waste of energy, and only leads to greater evils; therefore we should stamp out and exterminate all desire, all ambition, all enterprise, all hope of defeating evil; we should crush all our yearnings and longings and wants and submit, practice resignation, renunciation, meekness and submission, bow to fate— "Resist not evil." Evil is so omnipotent that resistance is madness. Existence is so ruled by evil that the only salvation lies in escaping from life back into the peaceful realm of death. Edwin Arnold, in "The Light of Asia," expresses it thus:

"The aching craze to live ends, and life glides
  Lifeless, to Nameless quiet, Nameless peace:
  Blessed Nirvana, sinless, stirless rest—
  The change that never changes."

And yet, this desire, which is the thing condemned by the Orientals, is regarded by Lester F. Ward, and all other great sociologists, as the mainspring of social progress. Without it no progress is possible. But, according to the religion of the Orientals, there is no triumph of religion until every possible tendency, every possible impulse, that could lead to progress, stimulating human advancement and the march of mind in the conquest of matter, has been stamped out, until progress cannot be possible in any direction; not until then have we reached the third truth: "Sorrow's Ceasing." The conclusion is: Life is not worth living; evil is triumphant; we must submit while we are here, and hope to get out of it as soon as possible.

This is the origin of the doctrine

of non-resistance of evil. No matter what evil may attack us we must bow in our helplessness and say with the Mohammedan, "It is Kismet"—it is fate.

The Christian religion, of which the mythical Matthew is an alleged exponent, is an Oriental religion. Some of us may have forgotten that, but it is none the less true. We have corrupted it with Western ideas; that it to say, we have improved it by injecting some civilization into it. But it is none the less Oriental in all its leading features. Its petrified sacred books are just as much opposed to change as are all sacred books and all things Oriental. What horrible hells have been prepared and threatened to those who ventured to make any addition to the knowledge contained in the Scriptures.

And the Hypatias, Bacons, Brunos and Ferrers who have dared to make any addition, and who have sought by the process of education to make their additions common property, have always found their Christian brothers ready to anticipate the so-called wishes of the Almighty and pay them installments of hell in advance.

The theory of non-resistance of evil is based on theological religion. It flies in the face of all modern science. Back of it stands the dogma that the Maker of All Things must be all-wise. If evil exists in the world it can only be by His permission. Not a sparrow can fall to the ground without His knowledge; not a hair on a human head be hurt without His consent. Therefore, if cities are decimated by the plague it can only be because He is willing it should be so. The plague is evil. Nobody disputes that. But shall it be resisted? Not according to the doctrine of "Resist not evil." According to that theory, sanitation, drains, whitewash, and chloride of lime are inventions of the devil. The plague cannot be there unless the powers that rule the universe desire it. Any sanitation is an attempt to thwart the desire of these powers. If the theory of non-resistance had not been set aside, and if men of science had not set themselves to resist the evil of the plague, the black plague, like the white plague, would be still among our visitors. Lightning which struck public buildings and laid them waste could not do so unless the Maker of the Universe consented. Benjamin Franklin, who attempted to resist with the lightning rod, was regarded as one of the advance agents of his Satanic Majesty.

The evils of disease and pain, supposed to have come into the world by the will of God, take various forms. Take the pain of women in childbirth, especially in extreme cases. That pain is evil. Shall we resist it? Or shall we, because it is a creation of the Almighty, allow it to go unresisted? Some men said: Resist! They tried anaesthetics for women in child-birth. And the theologians said it was another attempt to thwart the Almighty, and under no circumstances should it be permitted until Dr. Arthur Simpson Young presented the preachers an argument they could not answer. Dr. Young said: "You forget I am only imitating the Almighty Himself, who before He took the rib from Adam put him into a deep sleep."

The essential difference between science and religion gathers around this theory. Science believes in trying to conquer and abolish evil of all kinds. This is the supreme aim of science. It is the very breath of life of modern civilization. Religion, theological religion, on the contrary, with its cringing submission to evil, meets with defeat just in proportion as science advances and knowledge spreads. All through the centuries the attitude of non-resistance to existing evils has restrained the progress of the race. Science has been successful in the Occident; it has conquered, and it is pressing Christian theories to such an extent that the modern Christian cannot now even understand or comprehend his own doctrines. Where is the Christian who can see any sense, if he is smitten on one cheek, in turning the other to his assailant? Can you imagine a Christian in a restaurant running after a man who has taken his hat, to give him his coat?

Oriental ideas have become obsolete, the doctrine of non-resistance along with them. Only here and there do we find a really clever man, like Darrow, ready to inflict an Oriental quietism on the pulsing, throbbing life of the modern world.

Christianity is largely derived from Buddhism. The Christianity of the New Testament just as surely took its doctrine of "Resist not evil" from Buddhism as it took its personal devil from the superstition of Persia. This theory of non-resistance has passed from Buddha to Christ, from Christ to Tolstoy, and from Tolstoy to Darrow.

Sometimes a theory, born in one society under given social and material conditions, if transplanted to another country and a different material environment, will die out. But if there happens to be something in that environment which lends color to it, it may live on indefinitely. This is why the non-resistance theory of Christ reappears in the writings of Tolstoy. All Orientals have absolute monarchies. The monarch is all-powerful, and resistance to the evils of government is only another name for sudden death. The Jews of the time of Christ were so ruled by the Roman broadsword that resistance spelled extermination. And Christ gave the people the best advice he could have given them under the circumstances when he tried to persuade them not to resist. This condition is repeated in Russia, and it is chiefly for this reason that the theory reappears in Russia. The Russian autocracy is so supreme and powerful that to resist it is only a way to a sudden grave. So the theory of nonresistance keeps alive in Russia, because it happens to harmonize with social conditions there.

The great problem of America, and of Western Europe generally, is the problem of Capital versus Labor. We take our side with labor. Capital robs labor; and that robbery is evil. It is the crowning evil of the modern world. Shall we resist that evil? I say, yes. Darrow says, yes and no; practically, yes; theoretically, no. The truth of the matter is, there are two Darrows: A Mr. Hyde, of non-resistance; and a Dr. Jekyll, full of fight. These have both gone into print. Darrow, the Oriental poet and dreamer, wrote a book, entitled, "Resist not Evil." Darrow, the American citizen, ready at all times to help the laboring class resist any and all forms of evil that the ruling class may try to heap upon it, wrote a pamphlet: "The Open Shop." The motto of the pamphlet is: "The cause combatted for is yours. The efforts and sacrifices made to win it should therefore be yours." Darrow, the Darrow who wrote the pamphlet, is always engaged when the unions get into a tight corner. Why do you suppose they engage him? Because he is a non-resistant, and does not believe in resisting evils? No. They engage him, because they know that in spite of his acceptance of a dreamy, poetic theory he is as full of fight as a mountain lion, and will not give up until every weapon has been tried and the last possible blow is struck. I will read one or two passages from "The Open Shop." He says, speaking of unionism, that:

"Individually the man is helpless, the trade union has furnished the common workman the one institution to which he can look for friendship and protection; the one body on which he can rely for the redress of his grievances, and the protection of his rights, and if society were to remove that protection and safeguard, and cut the workman off from his fellows and leave him to fight his individual battles against the great combination of capital for which he works, it would leave the laborer stripped and naked to commence his long and painful journey back to serfdom once again, and when he starts out upon this road, the great mass of men whose independence has been won along with the workman's struggles, the great middle class, must go back with him."

If you resist not evil, or even if the unorganized worker resists alone, that means back to serfdom. This is the Darrow of the twentieth century. Again he says:

"The history of trade unionism—as, in fact, the history of the rise of the common people toward the measure of independence they now enjoy—is one long tale of struggles, defeats, and victories, and every single step in their progress has been against the most stubborn opposition and at the greatest cost."

There is little non-resistance here. He has the following to say about the "scab":

"The very reason that keeps men from

joining the unions of their craft makes them more servile and cringing to their employers; makes them ever subservient to his demands. They have learned well the lesson of the masters that to thrive you need only work hard and do all in your power to get the good opinion of your boss. So this class is ever ready to submit to encroachments; to take longer hours; to consent to poorer conditions; to make no trouble over unsafe tools, and to even let their wages be reduced."

According to this, non-resistance leads to disaster. These are the views of the fighting Darrow. Darrow, the non-resistant, has no say in this pamphlet.

In this debate you have your choice of two opposing philosophies. Mr. Darrow offers you the philosophy of the Orient; the philosophy of non-resistance; the philosophy of resignation, renunciation, helplessness, submission and despair—the philosophy of eternal stagnation. This philosophy of stagnation is the mental reflection of the stagnant life of Asia, and, in its turn, it acts as a preservative of the stagnation which gave it birth. Japan alone, of all the Asiatic nations, has broken this long trance and thrown off the paralyzing stupor; and this because she has responded to the example of those energetic, innovating, evil-resisting Westerners, who are still regarded by China as "foreign devils."

On the other hand, I offer you the philosophy of the Occident; a philosophy of the resistance of evil in all its forms. The offer is somewhat belated, as you have already accepted this philosophy. By it you regulate your daily lives. If you did not, civilization would drive you to the open

sky and a diet of roots and acorns.
My opponent himself has accepted
this philosophy of progress and action with all that part of his brain
which enables him to live and
breathe and maintain his being in the
metropolis of the Western world.
In the interior of his skull the theory
of non-resistance occupies only that
isolated corner where the convolu-
tions are less deep and more rudi-
mentary, the corner which is responsible for some of his literary produc-
tions.

In the days when we had not as
yet grasped the real significance of
the awakening of Japan we were
greatly alarmed by the "Yellow
Peril." Our alarm had its basis in
the fear that the East would overrun
the West; that the world would be
conquered by a race which would

offer no resistance to the evils of oppression and exploitation, a race that would slave from sunrise to sunset for a handful of rice.

In vain will my opponent endeavor to shake off this antithesis of Occident and Orient. You cannot travel backward upon the path that marks the genesis of his theory without discovering its Eastern birth. Darrow is a self-confessed disciple of Tolstoy. Tolstoy's country is on the borders of Cathay. Russia finds herself caught between white and yellow; and her perpetual problem is: Shall she stay back with the East or go forward with the West. Tolstoy and Darrow are, again, both disciples of an Oriental mystic, himself a mythical character, for whom the scenes are set at the eastern end of the Mediterranean, northeast of Egypt,

southeast of Turkey — further east
than either. The teachings, parables,
miracles and legends attributed to
him, and recorded in the New Testament, are an integral part of the in-
tellectual baggage of the dreamy,
credulous and uncritical East.

America, of all the Western countries, is the farthest removed from
the soporific influences and submit-
to-evil attitude of the Oriental, and
my opponent should have learned
long before this that his theory of
non-resistance to evil has no present,
nor any future, in this country. The
English poet, Tennyson, in "Locks-
ley Hall," contrasts these two posi-
tions, and like a true Westerner de-
cides for a progressive, evil-resisting
civilization, and against the intellec-
tual paralysis of Orientalism and sav-

agery. He begins by painting Oriental life in glowing colors and extolling its apparent advantages:

\* \* \* "Ah, for some retreat
Deep in yonder shining Orient where my
  life began to beat.

"There, methinks, would be enjoyment more
  than in this march of mind,
In the steamship, in the railway, in the
  thoughts that shake mankind.

"There the passions, cramp'd no longer,
  shall have scope and breathing space,
I will take some savage woman, she shall
  rear my dusky race.

"Iron-jointed, supple-sinewed, they shall
  dive, and they shall run,
Catch the wild goat by the hair, and hurl
  their lances in the sun;

"Whistle back the parrot's call, and leap the
  rainbows of the brooks,
Not with blinded eye-sight poring over miserable books."

Then our poet shakes himself out of his day-dream and swings back to the world of modern, progressive, social reality:

"Fool, again the dream, the fancy, but I KNOW my words are wild,
But I count the gray barbarian lower than the Christian child.

"I, to herd with narrow foreheads, vacant of our glorious gains,
Like a beast with lower pleasures, like a beast with lower pains!

"Mated with a squalid savage—what to me were sun and clime?
I, the heir of all the ages, in the foremost files of time.

"I, that rather held it better men should perish one by one,
Than that the earth should stand at gaze like Joshua's moon in Ajalon!

"Not in vain the distance beacons; forward, forward, let us range.

Let the great world spin forever down the
   ringing grooves of change.

"Men, my brothers; men, the workers, ever
   reaping something new,
That which they have done but earnest of
   the things which they shall do.

"Through the shadow of the globe we sweep
   into a younger day:
Better fifty years of Europe than a cycle of
   Cathay."

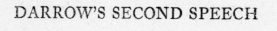

DARROW'S SECOND SPEECH

## DARROW'S SECOND SPEECH

As near as I can find out, the question with my opponent seems to hinge on a pedigree. I have seen some mighty poor things have good pedigrees. I never looked up the pedigree of non-resistance, and I do not care. It may have come from Asia, or from Africa, or from Europe. I do not know where it came from. I have an idea, though, that almost every prophet, and seer, and humanitarian the world over have always had a glimmering of this truth, and have taught it more or less in their philosophy, though they may not have practiced it. For it is one thing to believe a thing, and another to work at it. But they have seen this

vision, believed it, and wanted to
help it along, and looked forward to
the time when it shall be the rule,
I have no doubt whether in Europe
or in Asia. The real teachings of all
the great men in the world have not
been so much different, because after
all men's thoughts come from their
own conservativeness, what is inside
of them—not what is outside of
them. Two men see the same things,
and yet they think different thoughts.
That is due to the character of the
mind. Prophets the world over have
had rather similar thoughts, the
teachings of Buddha, Confucius,
Christ and the really great teachers
of the world have been wonderfully
alike, and where the doctrine came
from has nothing whatever to do
with it.

My friend tells you in one breath

that there is a small corner in my
brain where I believe in non-resistance—and from that I have written
this book. In the other he tells you
that he agrees with everything I have
said. Now, if he agrees with all I
have said on the subject of non-resistance, and all its inferences, then
all there is left is a question of definition. I do not care anything about
his definition, nor my definition.
And yet I think all men who have
claimed to believe in it have given it
the same definition. I have never
read that it meant that one could not
take a bath, or that one could not
cure himself of a disease, or could
not wear clean clothes. That has
nothing to do with non-resistance.

The doctrine of non-resistance is,
as a doctrine, opposed to force, violence, and punishment; and is a doc-

trine which teaches that the law of love is the right law of human action rather than the law of hatred, vengeance and punishment. You may say that you can carry this theory into plant and into animal life. But all this is largely in the realm of speculation. A man believes many things as to society, and as to human life that he cannot demonstrate, and that he can only see as visions before him of what he thinks a regenerated race will do, or some time become. You cannot apply it to all animal life, to all plant life, and to all human life, and say that if one individual should drop down into a society filled with strife and discord and combat he can live an ideal life and be governed by the rules which will one day govern the world. This fact in no way shows that this is the true rule of life, and in no way shows that the theory is the wrong theory.

Society today, as ever, is a mixture of the life of individual men. It is a mixture of the good and the bad, broadly speaking. It is a mixture of co-operation and competition; it is a mixture of hatred and fear; it is a mixture of war and peace. The world has evolved from the lowest order. It is still evolving. Is there any doubt with anybody who believes in evolution that as the human race evolves it will leave war, murder and bloodshed out; and that it will cling to co-operation, peace, and harmony, and love? If it does not do this, it will not evolve. That is what evolution means. Neither man individually, nor man mixed up in society, is able to demonstrate or exemplify this. All he can do is to go toward it, and be as sure as possible that he is on the right road, and that so far as in him lies he is helping the world to go the right road.

Maybe there are inconsistencies in this philosophy. It may be there are inconsistencies in those who preach it and talk it. Perhaps you can take some of my writings and find some that are inconsistent. I have talked too much to make it all consistent. But if you can find some inconsistent thing that I said you would have no more right to say that makes the theory wrong than to say Benjamin Franklin was a lunatic because he thought that he could keep off lightning with a lightning rod. That was a part of the witchcraft of science.

The theory is scarcely disputed by my friend—the theory, in all that it implies, is scarcely disputed. The theory has been promulgated as against the cruelty of society, as against the doctrine of "an eye for an eye, and a tooth for a tooth," which is prevalent.

He tells you this is the Christian doctrine that I am teaching. I wish it was. That is, I wish the Christian doctrine was this doctrine. Did you ever hear a preacher who preached it? Did you ever hear of an orthodox preacher who would not let go of the church before the jail? Would they give up punishment? Would they give up force? Don't they love the penitentiary more than the chapel? Did you ever know of one praying that a man should not be punished; or forgiving him his faults, or not criticising him for what they considered his errors? It is not the doctrine of the Christian church at all. It is the opposite. But if it is not the doctrine of the Christian church, neither is it the doctrine of China or Japan, except of a few of the wise, and great, and good, who there, as everywhere, saw what the rulers of the world have never seen, who felt what the cruel have never felt, whose minds had the imagination to feel the sufferings of their fellow men, whose hearts were so tender as to make them feel the heart throbs of the weak and poor and the suffering. But China, Japan, India, and the whole world have been ruled by hatred. They cut men's heads off in China. They send men to prison as punishment. The great religious teachers may have believed one thing, but their religious rulers have ever practiced another thing. Force is the essence of government. Every government upon the face of the earth has been over the protest of the weak and of the poor.

Almost all men in jail believe in non-resistance. In a way they are, generally, not wise and great. They have not had the time and the money to be wise and great. But all of them have an instinctive feeling as they look back at their lives that they have had to do just as they have done. They might look at the acts that placed them where they are, and into every one of the devious places that they have trod down from their cradles to the present, and they can see thousands of circumstances which held them in the grasp and made them what they are. And they know they are not to blame for their position. They know in their hearts that the whole theory of punishment is wrong, the whole theory, though it is the theory upon which the world goes today.

If Brother Lewis has been converted to the theory of non-resistance, in the penal code, I wish he would go to work and convert the rest of the world, for it needs it. There are only a few who have been converted to it. All the governments have been built upon it.

What is true of jails and penitentiaries is true of the state. Men have practiced force. They seem to forget that in the thousand activities of human life we go about our affairs automatically; that men turn to the right when they meet on the street, and that they go around each other the proper way. They live together automatically in most of the affairs of life. But they still seem to think that the great weight of the club, and the great power of the jail and prison, must be used or the state must fall to pieces. And so we build our armies and our navies, and make our penal statutes, and our cruel punishments, and the whole world believes in them—and the whole world practices them.

I believe with my friend that the great problem today is the problem of capital and labor. But how is that affected by the theory of non-resistance?

Those who think that non-resistance is a milk-and-water theory have got another guess. It is not. I was talking the other day with a man who had been a colonel in the war. I said: "I do not know how you could get up courage to go up in the face of cannons and bayonets and take your life in your hands." He says: "I did it, because I was too big a coward to run away." And that is why most all men go to war. They are too big cowards to stay at home. That is why men fight. They are too big cowards not to fight. Do you think it is a brave man who fights; or is it the brave man who does not fight? I will show you ten thousand men who are willing to go up in the face of hostile cannon, where you cannot find one man who will take one stick of criticism in a daily newspaper. There is not anything on earth so cheap as physical courage. Why even a bulldog can fight, but it has not got much brain. Fighting has nothing to do with the labor question, or with the question of capital and labor. How is it applied to the question as it exists today?

In order to change social conditions you say you must get rid of the ruling class, by force or some other way—one way or the other. Now, the weak are the poorest ones in the world to fight. They have no guns; the other fellow has them all. They have no organization. They have no chance in a fight. But they can fight. Workingmen of today can fight. If all of them would refuse to work or the great majority would refuse to work and enter into passive resistance—non-resistance—quit feeding the race; that is all you need to do. You cannot, of course. Wait until you can. You can get a small minority to arm themselves with brickbats and guns. What happens? You are sending a small force, poorly armed and equipped, against all the power of the state, and you cannot succeed, and you never have succeeded.

The only force that can win is determination, non-resistance, peaceable force. There is such a thing as peaceable force that is more forcible than forcible force.

Let me give you a few illustrations. What makes life? The cold, hard, stern winter; or the sunshine and the warm rain of the summer and the spring? The one means death, and the other means life. Repression and death go together. Love and sunshine and life are born together. Do you want to change the conduct of men, whether grown individuals or children; take a child and whip the child, can you change his conduct? You may change his conduct, but can you change his heart? Conduct is only the outward manifestation of the inward individual. To change the individual you must change the heart, and then the conduct must be free. Can you cure hatred with hatred? Everybody knows it in their own life. You may force men against their will to do certain things, but their hearts are a seething mass waiting for a time when they may accomplish other things by violence. Do you think you can do something for a man by sending him to the penitentiary? Gentleness is the law that makes life. Cruelty and hatred and coldness is the law that makes death. The question of non-resistance or resistance means a choice between those two laws.

# LEWIS' SECOND SPEECH

## LEWIS' SECOND SPEECH

Mr. Chairman, Mr. Darrow, Ladies
and Gentlemen:

I wish it to be clearly understood
that so far I have said nothing in-
tended to express any agreement with
Mr. Darrow as to the merits of the
theory of non-resistance; but I reas-
sert that I have no fundamental dis-
pute with my opponent on the subject of criminology.

The scientific method of treating
anything or any theory is the historical method. Many things which
remained mysteries for centuries became amazingly simple once their
origin became known. The question
of origin is now generally regarded
as the first and most important ques-

tion in the treatment of any scientific subject. And my friend Darrow proposes to sweep it away by a jibe about pedigrees. Scientific students will form their own estimate of his astonishing assertion that: "where the doctrine came from has nothing to do with it."

Mr. Darrow evidently believes that nobody ever supposed that Christianity, with its theory of non-resistance, meant the non-resistance of that form of evil called disease. The modern Christian will agree Darrow. He is a believer in baths and sanitation; but it was not always so. The founders of his religion regarded disease as due to the possession of devils as the New Testament amply shows. With them medical science counted for nothing and was discouraged. Their only cure for disease was an appeal to a being who had power to compel the devils to vacate human and other bodies. Medical science has only reached even its present unsatisfactory position in the teeth of theological opposition and the modern Christian has only accepted scientific theories of disease because they have been thrust upon him by the progress of knowledge—a progress that was bitterly fought by his historic church. Religious opposition to cleanliness and sanitation furnishes an instructive chapter in history—a chapter which my opponent has evidently left unread.

One of the chief arguments in Mr. Darrow's last speech, as in his first, is his assumption that the theory of non-resistance is a modern product— a crown and flower of recent thought.

The exact opposite is the truth. This theory belongs essentially to the ancient and primitive world. It has wide acceptance where evolution is unknown. It is as widely rejected in the modern Western world where the theory of evolution is solidly established.

Force, in the estimation of my opponent is always bad, and here I think he is wide of the truth. I will freely concede, and, if need be, maintain that the force used by a ruling class to oppress and rob a subject class, is evil. Such oppression and exploitation is very properly described as evil. This may be well described as aggression, and this class aggression is not a supposition; it is the central fact of present civilization. The question is: Should this evil be resisted? I say, yes. Such resistance is the life-breath of human progress, and non-resistance, as I have already shown by my opponent's own pamphlet, would lead us back to the dark ages. I am, as a Socialist, unalterably opposed to the aggression of a class, and a whole-hearted believer in resistance to that aggression. If a despotic nation seeks to tyrannize over a neighboring people because the neighbor is giving dangerous examples of the advantages of free institutions, while I would condemn the force so employed, I would applaud the force used by said neighbor if it should resist the tyranny. I am a believer in non-aggression, but opposed to the non-resistance of aggression. There is an important difference between non-aggression and non-resistance— a difference, however, which has played no part in the thinking of my opponent.

One of the points in my opponent's position seems to him to defy any contradiction. This is that whatever may be the practical shortcomings of his theory as remedy for present evils, at least it is ideally correct and will be the governing principle in the more enlightened society of the future. I regret being obliged to disappoint any expectations he may have of my acquiescence in this proposition. It is highly probable that society will not for some time rid itself of all forms of evil and of course the statement of the theory of non-resistance of evil implies existence of evil which is, or is not, to be resisted. I cannot conceive of a society in the future adopting as a working principle so suicidal a theory as the non-resistance of evil. Any society persisting in such a policy would eventually disappear in the struggle for existence. Unceasing resistance to evil in all its forms is the first condition of human progress.

A long and profound acquaintance with the practice of law has taught my opponent certain rather clever methods of getting out of tight places. And so we are calmly informed that there is a kind of force that is not forcible, and certain forms of resistance that do not resist. Passive resistance, for example, is not resistance at all, despite its being called such. It seems to my non-legal intellect that force which is not forcible cannot properly be called force, and the quality of resisting must be present in all forms of resistance whether it be called active or passive. Contradictions of terms may serve as argument in the courts but not in this debate.

It is a very excellent commandment which says: "Thou shalt not steal." Stealing is a form of aggression, especially when it is practiced by the strong against the weak; and the great bulk of real stealing is of this order. Darrow will admit that the stealing by the ruling class of the wealth produced by the working class is real stealing, and he is no doubt as willing as I am to say to that ruling class: "Thou shalt not steal." But suppose they ignore the injunction. What shall we do? Shall we allow their stealing to go unresisted? Our only course, it seems to me, is to fall back on the principle enunciated by Carlyle:

There are two guilty parties in any theft, the thief and the victim. If the robber pays no heed to our protest we must turn to the robbed worker and say: Thou shalt not be stolen from. People who allow themselves to be robbed when they could prevent it by resisting, have small claims to sympathy.

One of the aspects of non-resistance which damns the theory in my estimation is that it is so thoroughly in harmony with the desires of the ruling class. I cannot conceive that tyrants of any kind could wish anything better than that the evil of their oppression should go unresisted. It hardly seems probable that the existing possessing class will give up without a bitter struggle and a non-resistant working class would be doomed to perpetual slavery.

Mr. Darrow seems to regard the state as having existed almost from all eternity. He regards it as a product of savagery. In this he is altogether mistaken. If the anthropologists are to be believed, the state is only about five thousand years old, while primitive communism, which had no state, endured for approximately one hundred thousand years.

The state dates from the break-up of communal property and the beginning of private property in land. The principle of private property was extended to all means and modes of production as they developed and the state grew in power and importance as a consequence. Back of the state stands private property in the means of life. Capitalist property is the root from which the army, navy and police systems come forth. The state is a citadel built around capitalist property. The state is the grand weapon wielded against the workers whenever they grow restless under their heavy burdens.

Resistance to capitalist exploitation must begin at the state. The state, as a class instrument, must be wrested from the hands of its users, not to be used by its new owners to oppress others, but in order that it may be abolished. The abolition of the state is the historic task of the working class. This task can never be achieved by quiescence and non-resistance. It can only come as the result of long, hard struggle. This sense of the necessity for resistance is already part of the worker's mental processes. He cannot comprehend the meaning of non-resistance. The thing looks futile on the face of it.　He must fight back at all costs. The unions are founded on this idea. The future of the working class depends upon its ability to successfully resist oppression.　Liberty and struggle are inseparably linked together. A struggling, evil-resisting working class is indispensable to future progress of the human race.

# DARROW'S THIRD SPEECH

## DARROW'S THIRD SPEECH

I am not in the least interested in winning. It will make no difference to me who has the last speech, or who wins.

Now, it is very evident that my friend's definition of non-resistance and mine are not the same. Perhaps this will prevent this audience from getting its money's worth. I do not know. But if you get any ideas it does not make any difference.

I do not understand non-resistance to mean that you cannot fight disease, or destroy bedbugs, or take baths, or indulge in passive resistance. I do not think that anybody who has ever preached or taught non-resistance understood such a thing. Now, if

non-resistance does include it, then I
do not fully believe in non-resistance.
I do not propose to run a theory
down a blind alley just to hang on to
something.

I think a man is not obliged to
keep on working in order to practice
non-resistance. He can sit down and
rest if he wants to. And if all workingmen chose to sit down and rest,
instead of working to satisfy the
needs of the race, I would consider
that was passive resistance, non-resistance. I am not in the least re-
quired to work.

Neither will I admit that non-
resistance is a religious doctrine, except as the word "religion" might
mean something it has never meant
in practice. It might mean an aspi-
ration for a higher form of collective
life, which it has never meant. It

has always meant, a scheme for saving man's soul. But in that sense non-resistance has had nothing to do with it. Certainly these monks were not non-resistants. Because when the world was covered with the Dark Ages of religious belief and lack of intelligence, we had plenty of wars and plenty of Christianity. And the greatest wars the world has known have been fought on account of religious beliefs. Upon one side were the non-resistant Christians, and upon the other were the Mohammedans and other religious sects. It has never been any substantial part of the Christian religion. Now, of course, here and there great souls have been illumined with this thought and have taught it. But a religion is one thing, and a religious machine is quite another thing. And the religious machine has not only believed in resistance in this world but in the other, too; neither of which I believe in.

Whether non-resistance leads to pessimism does not interest me in the least. At least it is an open question. I believe the world is divided into two classes: the pessimists and the weak-minded. I am inclined to the pessimist side. But what that has to do with non-resistance I do not know.

My friend says he believes in non-aggression, but not in non-resistance. My friend is not a lawyer, but he acts like one.

When a couple of lawyers, twelve jurors, a judge, a bailiff, a lot of newspapers, and a religious public opinion send some poor devil to jail because he has stolen something society says they are practicing resistance to evil, because the man is a thief. My friend says that society is practicing aggression. From society's standpoint it is resistance to evil. It is dependent on the standpoint. I believe that is aggression. Society is engaged in what it believes resisting evil. They say, here is a man that has stolen something—violated some rule of the game—and we resist it by force, and we punish it. They call it resisting evil, and say it is wrong. It is wrong to commit aggression upon that man. If he stole, society is responsible, because under the arrangments of society that is the best profession he can get. Or else you might say with Mr. Lewis that evolution is responsible for it, on account of the way it shaped the skull, and the shape of the skull made the brain direct what he did. In any event, to harm a hair on his head, to inflict any pain or suffering upon the man, is wrong, and not conducing to the highest moral and physical development of the human race. The theory of resistance, and the practice of resistance of visiting force and violence and suffering upon your fellow man, is an evil theory, and can only produce evil results, near and remote, wherever you may find it.

He says the commandment "thou shalt not steal" is no more sacred than the commandment "Thou shalt resist stealing." It is just as incumbent on us not to permit stealing. True, under the moral code it is. But what are you going to do? Of course, nobody knows what stealing is. It is purely arbitrary. For a few men to fence off the earth and

for another man to go over inside
the fence and take something away
is stealing, under the rules of the
game. It is stealing from one man's
standpoint, but not from that of another. The men who fence off the
earth, they say the man who comes
over is the thief. Mr. Lewis says
the fellow who goes there should resist the other man. And society says,
the man who fenced off the earth
should resist the other man. It is
a question of standpoint. If you admit either philosophy, then both
have the right to resist, and it is a
question of force, and violence, and
punishment; and the question re-
solves down to this: under which
way can justice be the best and easi-
est obtained?

He says he believes in force for
the working class. It has always

been the same story since the world began, and will be so long as the world lasts. Who will win? Will it be the rulers, fitted and equipped with guns, ships, policemen, and with jails; always equipped for war? Or will it be the poor, the weak, and the disinherited, who have nothing to fight with?

I would not be so much opposed to force if I thought it would win. But I have seen that game tried so often that I know better. I think I know—that you cannot get justice that way. And suppose you could. Suppose the working class could turn society over, which they cannot—but suppose they could—and that they got the guns and cannons and swords, and they were the state, then what? Do you think they would do any better? I know them too well. Let me tell you. While the Socialist Party—I have nothing against that, except there are not enough of them vote the ticket— while they cannot muster a corporal's guard—every fellow wants to be the boss, and every fellow wants to make charges against every other fellow, and talk about him, lie about him, and gossip about him worse than a lot of women in a sewing society, and use all kinds of tactics to defeat him, and if they were running society they would not last as long as a snowball, not until they learn something. They would be just like the rest. They have got to learn that the whole campaign is wrong. They have got to learn that punishment is wrong; that resisting evil is wrong. They have got to learn the fundamental things, charity, humanity, brotherly love, which is the basis of all of it.

Do you think all the trades-unionists are angels? If you do, think it over again. They are not. There is a lot of them that are ignorant; some of them are brutal, and some of them are grafters.

Do you think if you stood society on its head, and gave them the guns, that all would be peace and harmony and loveliness; and that we would then practice non-aggression, if not non-resistance? No, you would be just where you were in the French revolution, where as soon as they got rid of the heads of the nobility they commenced cutting off each other's heads. It is what the whole thing leads to. It is in the theory of life as applied to the practice of man; to the doctrine they believe, and the life they live.

Do you believe in cruelty, in punishment? Do you use your tongue to condemn men and women? Do you use your efforts to get them in jail? Do you believe in punishment? If so, do you think your life and conduct conduces so well to civilization as the life and conduct of him who does not use his tongue and pen in that way? Or is the other theory right? Is the theory of love or hatred right?

My friend is wrong when he says that all strife comes from capitalism. It lurks in the human heart. It is part of the savage. It is in the beast, from there to man. You may go back to Egypt in the early scrolls and in their tombs and find the man with the spear, and the savage fights as much as the civilized. War comes from the brute, and if civilization means anything it means getting the brute out by teaching something higher.

My friend talks much about evolution. Of course I believe in evolution. Everybody does nowadays who has any sense, and that is not so very many. Is evolution war, or is it peace? Is the tendency toward war or peace? Why, the higher the race goes upwards, the more it co-operates. There is little co-operation in plant life; there is none, except one to feed upon another. There is little co-operation in animal life; little in the lower orders of man. And what men of vision and insight and inspiration are hoping for is the time when the human race will thoroughly co-operate, when each person will not be seeking only his own good, but the good of every other man. Evolution will not be complete until war and strife and competition are banished, and co-operation and love, and fellowship shall take its place.

# CLOSING SPEECH BY LEWIS

## CLOSING SPEECH BY LEWIS

Mr. Chairman, Mr. Darrow, Ladies and Gentlemen:

We are now informed that non-resistance is not a religious theory. Perhaps Mr. Darrow does not regard the New Testament, from which he took his text this morning, as a religious book, or Jesus Christ, the chief advocate of the theory, as a religious character, or Christianity as a religion. Whatever I may or may not have done I have clearly shown this theory to be an integral part of the religious systems of the Orient.

When workingmen are not satisfied with the terms offered by their employers they must decide what is

to be done. If they decide to stop
working their act is described by
Darrow as an instance of non-resistance. Darrow's claim cannot be sus-
tained. If the men decide not to
resist their employers they go on
working. They only strike when
they are determined on resistance
and, in their estimation, the strike is
a weapon used in a battle. My opponent can gain nothing by calling
this "passive resistance." So long
as it is resistance of any kind it belongs to my side of this argument.

Mr. Darrow freely admits that
society is the real aggressor in the
case of the criminal, and the real
evil is to be found in the behavior of
society. The question of non-resistance here is: Should the individual
who is denied an opportunity to live
honestly by vicious social laws re-

spect those laws and die without protest; or should he, claiming that life is above law, break through the meshwork and try to live despite the laws? According to the theory of non-resistance the individual in question should die quietly. Even Catholic theology is superior to this; the Catholic Church has always held that a starving person should steal both as a right and a duty. True, Catholics have perhaps never encouraged the practice of this precept except in the case of Cardinal Manning in the London dock strike.

Darrow would be willing for the working class to adopt force if he thought it would succeed. This is a frank admission of the validity of the argument I presented in my opening speech. Christ believed in non-resistance because He saw the

strength of Rome.  Tolstoy took the
same theory because the Russian
autocracy seemed impregnable. Darrow follows them in theory because
he believes that in a trial of strength
the workers would inevitably be
worsted by their masters.  Once
more we see, this time by Darrow's
confession, that the philosophy of
non-resistance is the philosophy of
despair.

I believe in resistance.  To me the
hope of the workers lies in the successful issue of the class struggle.
Not the despairing Tolstoy but the
courageous Marx has grasped the
principles which will carry the
workers to their desired goal.

The weakness of the working class
is apparent rather than real.  What
the workers lack is not strength but
intelligence.  The worker builds the

cities, runs the locomotive and the
steamship, maintains industry and
thereby feeds, clothes and houses the
inhabitants of the globe. Like At-
las, he carries the world on his shoul-
ders. His strength is moreover
steadily increasing. The capitalist
class on the other hand is degenerat-
ing. The great capitalists were in
many respects great men; but when
their sons realize that they are be-
yond economic want by reason of
papa's millions any strength or character that might have been forming
oozes away and they become "stage-
door Johnnies." The workers in the
final struggle will not measure
blades with the real organizers of
industry but with their purely para-
sitic, hare-brained and nerveless
descendants.

Social evolution is paving the way

for a new social order, an order in which there shall be no state because there will be no subject class to be kept down. That new order will owe its birth to the long travail of the working class; it will mark the culmination of a long story of resistance to the evils of class oppression. Then shall we close the first book of the history of the human race, a book saturated with the blood and tears of the workers of a thousand generations; we shall open a new volume and begin to write the first chapter of human liberty.

# THE MILITANT PROLETARIAT

**Austin Lewis**, already long recognized as one of the foremost Socialist writers in America, has now made what time will prove to be the most valuable American contribution to the literature of Socialism thus far produced. His new book, **The Militant Proletariat,** applies the fundamental principles of Socialism to the most recent economic and social developments. The great Socialist classics were written a generation or more ago. Marx prophesied the American trust. Now in all its fullness it is here. How is it to be met by the political and industrial organizations of the working class? For five years heated discussions have centered around this question. In **The Militant Proletariat** Austin Lewis presents the most valuable results of this discussion. No wide-awake Socialist will fail to read it. Cloth, 50 cents.

## CHARLES H. KERR & COMPANY,
### 118 West Kinzie Street, Chicago.